1595

D1377002

BOOKWORMS

Count On It!

Ten

Dana Meachen Rau

Marshall Cavendish
Benchmark
New York

Ten cups.

3

Ten blocks.

Ten paints.

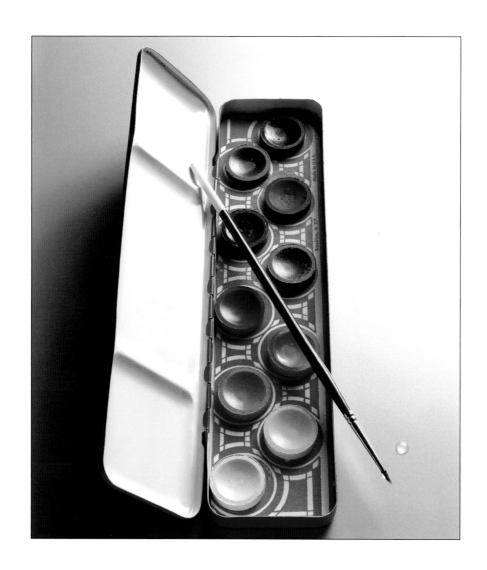

7

Ten socks.

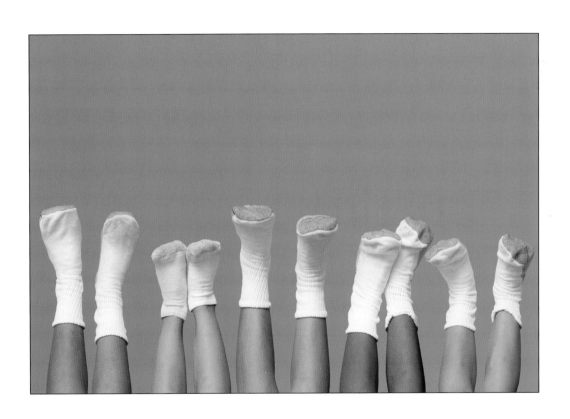

Ten birds.

Ten bows.

13

Ten fingers.

15

Ten toes.

Ten!

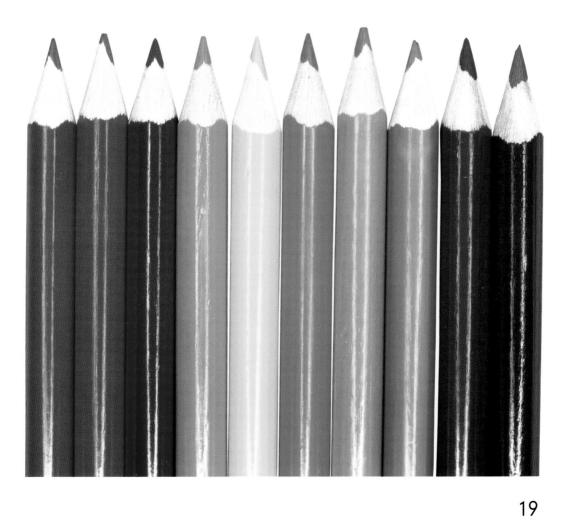

19

Words We Know

birds

blocks

bows

cups

fingers

paints

socks

toes

Index

Page numbers in **boldface** are illustrations.

About the Author

Dana Meachen Rau is the author of many other titles in the Bookworms series, as well as other nonfiction and early reader books. She lives in Burlington, Connecticut, with her husband and two children.

With thanks to the Reading Consultants:

Nanci Vargus, Ed.D., is an Assistant Professor of Elementary Education at the University of Indianapolis.

Beth Walker Gambro is an Adjunct Professor at the University of St. Francis in Joliet, Illinois.

Marshall Cavendish Benchmark
99 White Plains Road
Tarrytown, New York 10591-5502
www.marshallcavendish.us

Library of Congress Cataloging-in-Publication Data

Rau, Dana Meachen, 1971–
Ten / by Dana Meachen Rau.
p. cm. — (Bookworms. Count on it!)
Summary: "Identifies objects that inherently come in tens and lists other examples"—Provided by publisher.
Includes index.
ISBN 978-0-7614-2971-5
1. Ten (The number)—Juvenile literature. 2. Number concept—Juvenile literature. I. Title. II. Series.
QA141.3.R28 2009
513—dc22
2007024615

Editor: Christina Gardeski
Publisher: Michelle Bisson
Designer: Virginia Pope
Art Director: Anahid Hamparian

Photo Research by Anne Burns Images

The photographs in this book are used with permission and through the courtesy of:
Corbis: pp. 1, 19 Lili K./zefa; pp. 13, 20BL Bloomimage; pp. 15, 21TL Tom Grill; pp. 17, 21BR Ted Horowitz.
Jay Mallin Photos: pp. 3, 9, 20BR, 21BL. SuperStock: pp. 5, 20TR age fotostock. Jupiter Images: pp. 7, 21TR.
Animals Animals: pp. 11, 20TL.

Printed in Malaysia
1 3 5 6 4 2

DATE DUE

OCT 0 5 2013			